THE FANTASTIC
FERRIS WHEEL

The Story of Inventor George Ferris

Betsy Harvey Kraft

illustrated by **Steven Salerno**

Christy Ottaviano Books

HENRY HOLT AND COMPANY ✦ NEW YORK

For Lindsay and Julia
—B. H. K.

For my beloved grandparents, Rose and Leon. As little kids,
they probably first rode a Ferris wheel in 1917.
—S. S.

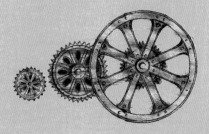

Henry Holt and Company, LLC, *Publishers since 1866*
175 Fifth Avenue, New York, New York 10010 • mackids.com

Henry Holt® is a registered trademark of Henry Holt and Company, LLC.
Text copyright © 2015 by Betsy Harvey Kraft
Illustrations copyright © 2015 by Steven Salerno
Image on the title page and page 40: The Ferris wheel at the World's Columbian Exposition of 1893
in Chicago (b/w photo), American photographer (19th century), Private Collection/Bridgeman Images.

Henry Holt books may be purchased for business or promotional use. For information on
bulk purchases, please contact the Macmillan Corporate and Premium Sales Department at
(800) 221-7945 x5442 or by e-mail at specialmarkets@macmillan.com.

Library of Congress Cataloging-in-Publication Data
Kraft, Betsy Harvey.
The fantastic Ferris wheel : the story of inventor George Ferris / Betsy Harvey Kraft ;
illustrated by Steven Salerno. — First edition.
pages   cm
Summary: "The story of George Ferris, inventor of the iconic Ferris wheel" —Provided by publisher.
Audience: Ages 5 to 9.
ISBN 978-1-62779-072-7 (hardcover)
1. Ferris, George Washington Gale, 1859–1896—Juvenile literature. 2. Inventors—United States—Biography—Juvenile literature.
3. Structural engineers—United States—Biography—Juvenile literature. 4. Ferris wheels—History—Juvenile literature.
5. World's Columbian Exposition (1893 : Chicago, Ill.)—Juvenile literature. I. Salerno, Steven, illustrator. II. Title.
TA140.F455K73 2015   791.06'80284—dc23   2014044914

First edition—2015 / Designed by Patrick Collins
The artist created the original illustrations for this book with crayon, ink, gouache, and pastel on paper. After scanning the
drawings, he layered and arranged them into their final compositions using Adobe Photoshop, with additional coloring applied.
Printed in China by RR Donnelley Asia Printing Solutions Ltd., Dongguan City, Guangdong Province

1 3 5 7 9 10 8 6 4 2

Make no little plans.
They have no magic to stir men's blood....
Make big plans; aim high in hope and work.

—DANIEL BURNHAM,
a Chicago architect and chief of construction
for the 1893 Chicago World's Fair

A long time ago—more than one hundred years, in fact—a young boy lay in the grass, thinking. *That waterwheel. It goes round and round and up and down.* The current from a nearby stream made the wheel move. The boy watched, fascinated. *Maybe there is another way to make a wheel go around,* he thought.

Many years later the boy, George Ferris, became an engineer. He now designed bridges and buildings and roads made of steel and concrete. But he still had wheels on his mind. He visited Chicago, the city getting ready for a giant world's fair known as the Columbian Exposition of 1893.
It would open in the spring.

Architects were designing elaborate buildings for the fair's exhibits and performances. Musicians were writing special music. Artists painted glorious pictures, and sculptors carved giant statues.

Almost every country in the world planned to show off its creations at the event. There were buildings devoted to the latest inventions in manufacturing, farming, and transportation. One building featured new developments in the field of electricity: stoves and elevators, telephones, phonographs. Most impressive, though, were the displays of electricity used for lighting. This was a dramatic advance in science. The entire fairgrounds would be illuminated by an array of lights, large and small. This would be one of the most exciting attractions of the fair.

There were plans for beautiful parks and small lakes, called lagoons, with boats for tourists. For three dollars, people could ride in a hot air balloon. Different countries would create villages showing off their cultures. There would be camels and elephants—even a belly dancer from Egypt. Visitors from Europe, Asia, and Africa would be there. The fair was going to be grand!

The men and women in charge of the fair wanted something special for Chicago to draw people to the event. Something no one had ever seen before. Something no one could imagine. They were not sure what it would be, but it needed to be spectacular.

George Ferris met with other engineers in Chicago. Daniel Burnham, one of the men in charge of planning the fair, spoke to the group and challenged the American engineers to come up with extraordinary ideas.

Be more creative, he insisted. Just three years earlier, a French engineer named Gustave Eiffel had designed a special tower for France's 1889 World's Fair. Built of more than 8,000 tons of iron, the tower soared more than 984 feet (300 meters) above the Paris fairgrounds. People came from all over the world to see the Eiffel Tower.

"Think no little thoughts," Burnham told the group. "Make big plans." America's engineers were on the spot. But all their ideas seemed silly or impractical.

984 feet (300 meters)

8,000 tons of iron

After hearing Burnham's challenge, George Ferris began to dream, plan, and design. Maybe he even remembered the waterwheel from his younger days. A few weeks later, while talking with some engineer friends, he pushed a piece of paper across the table.

His friends looked at the sketch he had drawn. It was a huge circle surrounded by a web of delicate lines. Next to the drawing were notes, numbers, and more drawings.

"What is it?" they asked, puzzled.

"It's an observation wheel for the World's Fair," he answered excitedly.

"Hmmm," his friends murmured.

"From the wheel, people can observe, or see far into the distance," he explained.

His friends knew about observation wheels. They were small, wooden contraptions sometimes seen at carnivals or local fairs. But the one George was showing them looked enormous.

They studied his drawing more closely. Were those passenger cars attached to the wheel? People would actually ride on this towering thing? *George must be out of his mind*, they thought.

In June 1892, George showed his design to the organizers of the fair. "There's never been anything like it," he told them.

The wheel would rise 264 feet (80.5 meters) into the air, the height of a twenty-six-story building. Thirty-six passenger cars would hang from the rim of the wheel. Each car would hold sixty riders as they circled high above the fairgrounds. The power for the wheel would come from two 1,000-horsepower steam engines.

The fair organizers examined the plans carefully. The wheel would be unique, they agreed. Unlike the Eiffel Tower in Paris, it would move. It certainly would attract people's attention.

But it would be way too dangerous. It was a "monstrosity," one man said. What if it collapsed with two thousand people on it? Or what if a big wind came along and blew it down?

"I'm an engineer," George said. "I will make sure the wheel is perfectly safe."

The members of the fair committee said yes, George could build his wheel. But the next day they changed their minds. It just seemed too risky.

No matter, George remained determined. He spent thousands of dollars of his own money to make his plans more detailed. He persuaded wealthy investors to help fund the building of the wheel as there was no money in the fair's budget to pay for the project. In November, Daniel Burnham again turned down George's proposal. But he agreed to show it to other members of the committee.

Finally, on December 16, 1892, the fair committee said yes. "Go ahead and build your crazy wheel," they told him. "But make sure it's safe. And hurry. The fair opens to the public in four and a half months."

26 stories

264 feet (80.5 meters)

36 cars (60 riders each)

Chicago is known for its cold weather. But the winter of 1892 to 1893 was one of the worst ever. Bitter winds blew in from Lake Michigan. Blizzards dumped layers of snow and ice on the fairgrounds. The temperature dropped to freezing. Then it dropped to below freezing. Then it dropped to below zero. Workers blasted through the frozen fairgrounds using dynamite.

The cold was not the only problem. Workers had to dig deep into the earth before they found solid ground. They crisscrossed steel bars at the bottom of the giant hole. They worked for weeks in the bitter cold, pouring layers of concrete on top of the steel. The heavy wheel would be supported by solid towers, which required a firm foundation.

George needed more than 100,000 different parts to build the wheel. Some were tiny. Some were enormous. Railroad cars from all over the United States chugged their way to the Chicago fairgrounds. The cars carried screws, bolts, and steel bars. Engineers checked all the parts to make sure every one was perfectly crafted. Groups of workers carefully pieced the parts together. Each had to fit *exactly* into the right place.

As the weather in Chicago grew warmer, George's strange-looking creation began to rise above the fairgrounds. People craned their heads to see. It looked like two gigantic bicycle wheels hanging forty feet apart. Steel braces and wires connected the two wheels. A heavy iron pole, called an axle, ran through the centers of the wheels, joining them.

"Look at that," people said as they gazed up.

"Looks like a spiderweb," one person said.

Folks were not sure what to think of George's invention.

On May 1, 1893, the fair opened to the public. Thousands of excited men, women, and children poured through the entrance gates. Some came from downtown Chicago, traveling by boat across part of Lake Michigan. Some arrived by train. Others walked or rode bicycles.

Visitors from around the world marveled at the attractions. They were dazzled by the fair and hundreds of new sights.

While George's big wheel was not yet finished, it was still the talk of the town. Some people were terrified just looking at it. Others couldn't wait to ride on it.

But would it work the way it was supposed to? Would it rise into the sky, then glide gently down again? Would it be steady? Would it be safe?

Finally the wheel was ready for a test run. Spectators on the ground waited anxiously as construction workers jumped onto the bars of the wheel. Steam from the engines rushed through underground pipes and sent the giant wheel slowly rotating. The workers and engineers held on and yelled with excitement as they sailed in a giant circle toward the sky and back down again. Watchers below cheered. It would not be long before fairgoers could ride on the wheel.

The fair managers were relieved. The wheel seemed safe—so far. Without passengers, the wheel weighed more than 1,000 tons. Would it still be safe with the added weight of thirty-six passenger cars carrying more than two thousand people?

In late June, the wheel opened to the public. A throng of children and adults lined up to buy tickets. Each paid fifty cents for the ride. They stepped onto a loading platform and waited next to the rim of the giant wheel. The passenger cars gleamed with fresh green paint, polished wooden doors, and glossy brass trim. Conductors, dressed in blue-and-white uniforms with white gloves, pulled open the doors to the cars. The crowds rushed forward. Each car had large glass windows so the passengers could view the landscape below.

The engines throbbed as the wheel began to move. There was no turning back now. Up, up they glided. When each car stopped at the top, riders hung suspended above the ground. They were almost as high as the Statue of Liberty in New York City's harbor—and higher than Chicago's tallest skyscraper.

For twenty minutes the riders circled in the air, making stops to load more passengers or let them off. From here they could see the entire city of Chicago, its suburbs, the blue expanse of Lake Michigan, and parts of Wisconsin, Michigan, Illinois, and Indiana. The view was astounding.

The ride *had* been the thrill of a lifetime. One thrill was enough for some folks; others raced to the end of the ticket line for another ride.

Thousands of visitors rode the wheel on that first day. And soon it was the most popular attraction at the Chicago World's Fair. Rides were especially popular in the evening. As the sun set in the west, passengers could see its golden reflection on the waters of Lake Michigan. They saw the tiny network of Chicago's streets and rooftops stretched out beneath them.

And as the sky faded to a dark blue, three thousand electric lights strung along the wheel turned on, making the night seem magical.

George's wheel was an enormous success.

On July 9, the weather in Chicago was very hot. The sun beat down on the thousands of visitors who raced through the gates of the fair. But at three o'clock that afternoon, the sun vanished from the sky.

"Look at that," someone said nervously as storm clouds gathered in the sky. A violent wind began to blow. A gust lifted one of the boats from the lagoon and tossed it back into the water, upside down.

The operators of the hot air balloon decided it was getting too dangerous to send the balloon up and stopped selling tickets.

People on the ground anxiously eyed George's wheel. Surely the operators would close it down too. But the wheel kept loading passengers. More dark storm clouds appeared. Passengers already on board watched nervously as a tornado funnel formed and headed toward the fairgrounds.

Passengers gasped as they saw tents on the ground pull up their stakes and flap wildly in the wind. Beneath them they saw burly men struggling to hang on to the cable that anchored the hot air balloon to the ground. They watched in terror as the tornado shredded the balloon's silk fabric.

Riders on the wheel heard the sound of breaking glass. The wind had blown panels from one of the fair's main buildings and shattered them into thousands of pieces.

People on the ground ran for cover. One woman on the wheel fainted.
Others prayed for their lives as the wind howled around them.

This was the storm everyone had dreaded. Gale-force winds rose to
115 miles per hour. *The wheel will collapse,* people worried. The flimsy
spokes could snap. Or the passenger cars might blow right off the wheel.
Now, as everyone watched the storm rage across the fairgrounds, they
feared the worst.

A newspaper reporter wrote that when the storm began, George Ferris, along with his wife, hurried to the wheel and entered one of the cars. "As the mad storm swept round the cars, the blast was deafening," the reporter wrote. "It screamed through the thin spider-like girders and shook the windows with savage fury." But "the inventor had faith in his wheel," he continued. "The beautiful wheel hardly shivered." It turned, he wrote, as evenly and smoothly as if it were in a mild breeze.

Many of the buildings and attractions at the fair were badly damaged from the storm. But the Ferris wheel stood unscathed. And the inventor, George Ferris, became even more well known than he already was.

Hundreds of famous people visited the fair during the summer months of 1893. Harry Houdini performed his magic tricks near the wheel's location. It's likely he took time off from his act for a ride.

Theodore Roosevelt, who would become president of the United States a few years later, stopped at the fair to have lunch with Daniel Burnham. There is no record of Roosevelt riding the Ferris wheel, but given his love of exciting new experiences, he would have been thrilled if he did.

Harry Houdini

Teddy Roosevelt

Chief Standing Bear, leader of the
Ponca Native American tribe, rode
the wheel wearing a full headdress
made of two hundred
colorful feathers.

Chief Standing Bear

Fourteen-year-old
Helen Keller took a ride.
She could neither see
nor hear, but she could
sense the excitement of
the crowd and feel
the big wheel carry
her gently up and
then down again.

Helen Keller

George's Ferris wheel brought thousands of visitors to the Chicago World's Fair. When the fair closed in October, more than one and a half million people had ridden it. And it continued to circle! First the wheel was moved to a spot in one of Chicago's busy neighborhoods. Yet business was slow, and it was soon sold to the city of St. Louis. At the St. Louis World's Fair in 1904, the wheel once again thrilled thousands of visitors. But when that fair ended, there was unfortunately no new home for the wheel. It was destroyed with dynamite and sold for scrap.

George Ferris's design and vision still live on.
Observation wheels everywhere are now called Ferris
wheels in his honor. Engineers continue to build taller
and taller structures based on his original design.

The London Eye
England, 2000

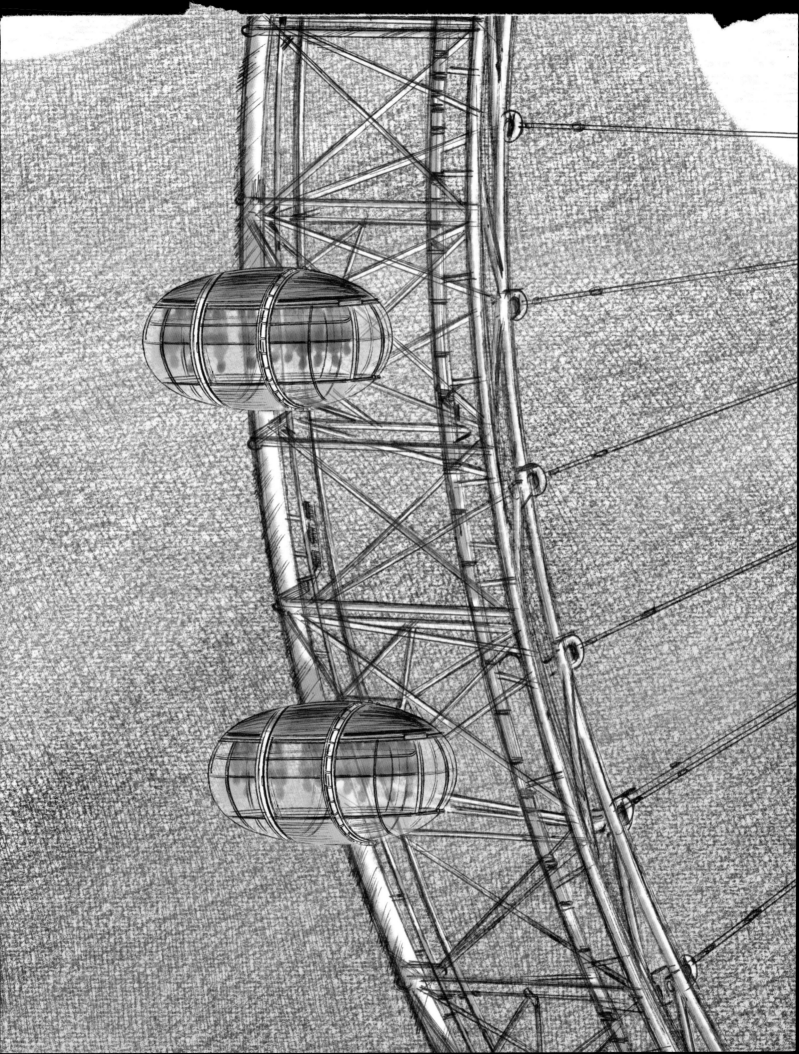

Perhaps the seeds of the extraordinary wheel came to George as he lay in the grass as a boy, watching the waterwheel turn. As long as there are dreamers like George Ferris ready to make big plans, the world can look forward to wondrous new inventions like his.

More About George Ferris

GEORGE WASHINGTON GALE FERRIS JR. was born on February 14, 1859, in Galesburg, Illinois, a small frontier town in the Midwest. He and his eight brothers and sisters lived on a large family farm.

When George Jr. was five, the family moved west to Nevada. There the family built a big ranch for animals and crops. The land was dry, and they irrigated the ground to provide water for the thirsty fields. George Jr. was fascinated as he watched all the construction going on—canals, culverts, farm buildings, and bridges.

When he was seventeen, George went to the Rensselaer Polytechnic Institute in Troy, New York, to learn engineering. After graduation, he helped design and build bridges and tunnels. He became an expert on large structures and the quality of steel.

The fair was organized to celebrate the four hundredth anniversary of Christopher Columbus's discovery of America. It was officially called the 1893 Columbian Exposition. Most people referred to it simply as "the fair" or "the exposition."

After the success of the wheel at the fair, engineers at another firm claimed *they* had designed one that operated the same way. They said George had stolen their idea, and they sued him. After several months of wrangling, the case was settled. George's design was unlike anything built before, the judges agreed.

No one has ever discovered the original drawings for George's invention, and he never patented his plans for the wheel. He once said the drawings he showed his friends at dinner in Chicago were complete and that he never changed them.

"I got out some paper and began sketching," he said. "I fixed the size, determined the construction, the number of cars we would run, the number of people it would hold. . . . In short, before the evening was over, I had sketched out almost the entire detail and my plan never varied an item from that day on."

Others wanted to copy George's success. They built their own wheels in Europe and elsewhere, using George's design. In 2000, a huge wheel called the London Eye opened in England. It was then the tallest wheel in the world, at 446 feet. In 2008, the Singapore Flyer opened in Asia, towering at 541 feet. And there are plans for new, even taller wheels in cities across the globe.

George Ferris's contribution to the world of engineering continues today, still bearing his name and the results of his extraordinary vision.

Sources

Hyde Park Historical Society, Chicago, Illinois (hydeparkhistory.org)

Larson, Erik. *The Devil in the White City: Murder, Magic, and Madness at the Fair that Changed America.* New York: Vintage Books, 2003.

Lawson, Robert. *The Great Wheel.* New York: Walker Children's Books, 2004.

Library of Congress newspaper archives (chroniclingamerica.loc.gov)

Peck, Richard. *Fair Weather.* New York: Puffin, reprint 2003.

Shaw, Marian. *World's Fair Notes: A Woman Journalist Views Chicago's 1893 Columbian Exposition.* St. Paul, MN: Pogo Press, 1992.

Weingardt, Richard. *Circles in the Sky: The Life and Times of George Ferris.* Reston, VA: American Society of Civil Engineers, 2009.